Treasure Hunter's Handbook

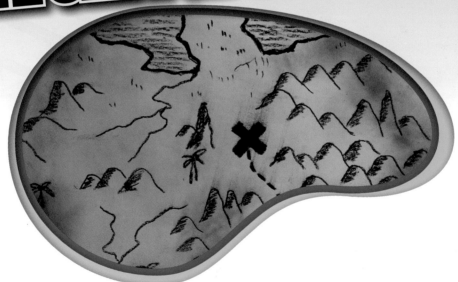

Anna Claybourne

Published 2011 by
A&C Black Publishers Ltd.
36 Soho Square, London, W1D 3QY

www.acblack.com

ISBN   HB 978-1-4081-3370-5
       PB 978-1-4081-3365-1

Text copyright © 2010 Anna Claybourne

This book is produced using paper that is made from wood grown in managed, sustainable forests. It is natural, renewable and recyclable. The logging and manufacturing processes conform to the environmental regulations of the country of origin.

Produced for A&C Black by Calcium. www.calciumcreative.co.uk

Printed and bound in China by C&C Offset Printing Co.

All the internet addresses given in this book were correct at the time of going to press. The author and publishers regret any inconvenience caused if addresses have changed or sites have ceased to exist, but can accept no responsibility for any such changes.

Acknowledgements

The publishers would like to thank the following for their kind permission to reproduce their photographs:

Cover: Shutterstock
Pages: Corbis: Lebrecht Authors/Lebrecht Music & Arts 13, Sanford/Agliolo 20; Dreamstime: Daniel Korzeniewski 9; Photos.com: 18t, 18b; Shutterstock: Noam Armonn 10, cbpix 21, Eric Isselée 5, Jocicalek 16, Konstantynov 12, Dudarev Mikhail 11, Myotis 15, PeppPic 19, Micha Rosenwirth 14, Sakala 4, Maksim Schmeljov 8, James Steidl 6, Werg 17, Robb Williams 7.

Contents

Be a Pirate!

Pirates were scary people who sailed the seas. They looked for treasure to steal.

A pirate's life for me

If you want to be a pirate, this book will tell you how.

Aaarr, me hearties

Pirate parrot

Pirates sometimes kept a parrot as a pet.

Make sure you do what the **captain** says!

The Pirate Ship

You will need a pirate ship. It must be small and fast – so it can catch other ships.

Get to work!

To look after your ship you must:

1 Scrub the **decks.**
2 Mend the **sails.**

Keep your ship clean!

Fly the flag

Pirate ships had scary **flags** to frighten people.

Sail

Hop on board

Pirate Rules

The **crew** of the pirate ship chooses who will be captain. Maybe it will be you...

Be a good pirate

You must follow these rules:

1 Don't fight **on board**.
2 Share your food.
3 Share any treasure.

Lovely gold

Don't cheat

Never trick your pirate crew. They will leave you all alone on an island.

Gold

This **loot** is for sharing.

Sailing Tips

How will you know which way to sail? Look at stars and the sun to find your way.

On the map

You can also use a **map** to sail the seas. Mark it with your best treasure-hunting spots.

Use a **telescope** to look for land.

Buried treasure

Pirates made treasure maps to remember where they buried their loot.

Telescope

Land ahoy!

Into Battle

Have you spotted a treasure ship? Then it's time to attack! Sail up to the ship, and leap aboard.

Fighting gear

You will need:

- A sword called a cutlass.
- A pistol – this is a small gun.
- An **axe** is useful too.

Pirates had lots of **weapons**.

Walk the plank

Pirates made the other ship's crew walk along a **plank** into the sea.

Plank

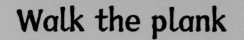

Sword

Give me your loot!

13

Treasure Tricks

Now you can get your hands on the ship's treasure! You might find gold, silver, or **precious** stones.

Bury your treasure

To keep treasure safe you should:

1 Bury it on a **desert island.**
2 Make a map showing where you buried it.

A desert island – perfect for burying loot.

Pirate coins

Coins were made of gold or silver. Pieces of eight were silver coins.

Treasure island

Pirate Food

Most pirate ships carried biscuits and beans on board. But you'll have to catch fish to eat too.

Cook like a pirate

To make a stew:

1 Put some meat, fish, eggs, or beans in a cooking pot.
2 Add some water, and cook.

Anyone for fish fingers?

Munching maggots

Watch out for maggots.
They love to eat
beans and biscuits.

What a catch!

Lost a Leg?

Pirate battles are dangerous. You could lose an eye, a hand, or a leg!

Chop, chop!

If your arm or leg is badly hurt, you might have to chop it off. But you can use a wooden leg or a handy hook instead.

Wooden leg

A wooden leg and a hook.

18

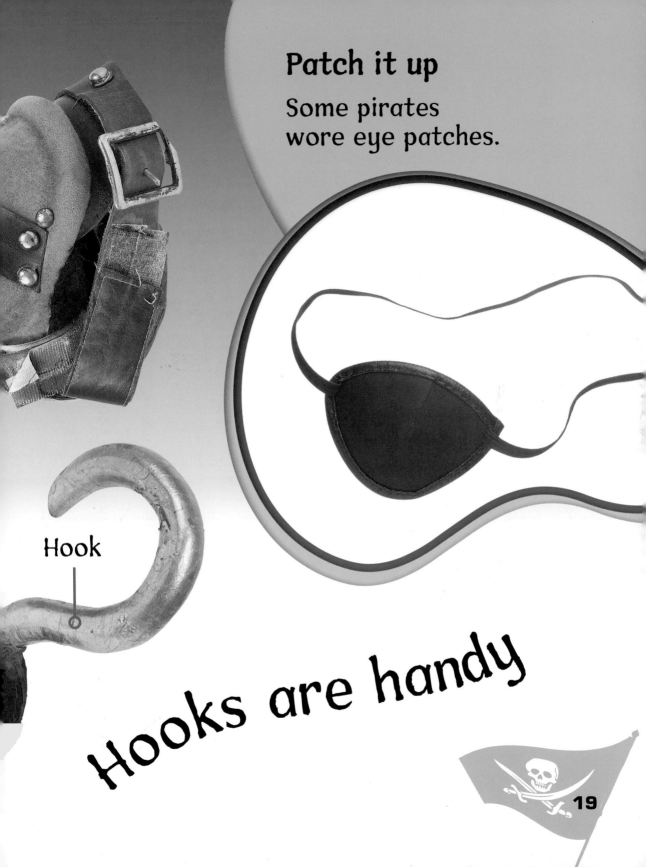

Patch it up

Some pirates
wore eye patches.

Hook

Hooks are handy

Caught at Last!

Being a pirate is tough. Your ship could sink, or you could be caught and sent to **prison**.

Help!

If your ship does sink, you might have to jump into the sea and swim for dry land.

Hold on – it's rough at sea!

Shark attack

Watch out for sharks.
They follow ships looking
for food. That could be you!

Good luck!

Glossary

axe sharp piece of metal on a wooden handle

captain person who is in charge of a ship and its crew

crew pirates and sailors who work on a ship

decks outdoor floor area of a ship

desert island island where no one lives

flags pieces of material with patterns or pictures

loot money, jewels, or other things that pirates steal from ships

map drawing that shows where places are

on board on a boat or a ship

plank long piece of wood

precious worth lots of money

prison place where some people who have broken the law are locked up

sails big pieces of material that catch the wind to push a boat forwards

telescope tool that makes faraway things look closer

weapons tools used for fighting

Further Reading

Websites

Try the word games and quiz about pirates at:
www.learnenglishkids.britishcouncil.org/category/general-themes/pirates

Read a pirate adventure story at:
www.nationalgeographic.com/pirates/adventure.html

Books

Pirate Poems by David Harmer, Macmillan (2007).

See Inside Pirate Ships by Rob Lloyd Jones, Usborne (2007).

Stories of Pirates (Young Readers) by Russell Punter, Usborne (2003).

Index